New and Selected Poems

New and Selected Poems

BY TONY CONNOR

London
Anvil Press Poetry

Published in Great Britain in 1982
by Anvil Press Poetry Ltd
69 King George Street
London SE10 8PX
ISBN 0 85646 069 9

Copyright © 1982 by the University of Georgia Press
Athens, Georgia 30602

Set in 10 on 12 point Monticello type
Printed in the United States of America

This book is published
with financial assistance from
The Arts Council of Great Britain

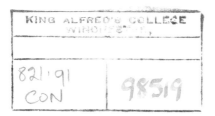

Acknowledgments

The poems in Part I are drawn from four volumes now out of print: *With Love Somehow* (London: Oxford University Press, 1962), *Lodgers* (London: Oxford University Press, 1965), *Kon in Springtime* (London: Oxford University Press, 1968), and *In the Happy Valley* (London: Oxford University Press, 1971). My other volume, *The Memoirs of Uncle Harry* (London: Oxford University Press, 1974), consists of one long sequence, the individual parts of which only reveal their point and purpose in relation to the whole. Of the new poems, a large group appeared in *Malahat Review* (no. 56) together with an essay on my work by Larry P. Vonalt. Other poems appeared in *College English* and *Poetry Northwest*. "Bringing in the Houseplants," "Emptying the Fishtank," and "Reminiscences Remembered" appeared in *Poetry*.

T. C.

Contents

II · New Poems

I

Selected Poems

A Rather Public Statement

I do not intend to contribute
a single line, any half-heard
snatch of mystery
to the street's chronicle.
I am deaf among men,
I am dumb among women,
I am the prince of never-there,
the master of winter.

I have no knowledge to offer
about the marriage bed,
nor am I able to say
where, or why important
decisions were made
affecting the lives
of all who heard them
and many more who did not.

I will not pretend an ability
to judge character from faces;
darkness frightens me
and I am apprehensive in sunlight.
Nevertheless,
mine was the bland smile,
the fur coat of incomprehension
in the catastrophe.

When the trek ended, frustrated
by the abattoir wall,
and the disgusted others
started rewinding the string,
I was in the chip shop

ordering fourpenn'orth.
I had not come all that way
for nothing.

On certain nights I have discerned
complicated patterns
in smudged penumbras,
but have never missed my supper.
The voices from alleys
—loving or hating—
I have accepted as part
of a wholesome definition.

You will appreciate my reluctance
to give you directions:
my inability to reach
the homes of others
is widely known—
although one of my hobbies
is studying maps
in the front room.

Finally, let me assure those
who imagine my lending a willing ear,
that my lopsided appearance
is congenital,
and should not be interpreted
as a leaning
towards anything
other than the ground.

4

End of the World

The world's end came as a small dot
at the end of a sentence. Everyone died
without ado, and nobody cried
enough to show the measure of it.

God said, "I do not love you," quite
quietly, but with a final note.
It seemed the words caught in his throat,
or else he stifled a yawn as the trite

phrase escaped his dust-enlivening lips.
At least there was no argument,
no softening tact, no lover's cant,
but sudden vacuum, total eclipse

of sense and meaning. The world had gone
and everything on it, except the lives
all of us had to live: the wives,
children, clocks which ticked on,

unpaid bills, enormous power-blocks
chock-full of arms demanding peace,
and the prayerful in a state of grace
pouncing on bread and wine like hawks.

Mrs. Root

Busybody, nosey-parker,
lacking the vast discretion of most
was this woman. The self-cast
chief mourner at funerals, worker
at weddings, she could sniff out death
in a doctor's optimism, joggle
a maiden's mind (button-holed on the front path)
till virginity bit like filed teeth.

Prepared, without discrimination,
friend and enemy for the grave:
washed and talcumed them all. This woman,
who wore such ceremonies like a glove,
could console a grief-struck household
that hardly knew her name, and then
collect money for a wreath fit to wield
at a Queen's passing. Death-skilled

but no less wedding-wise,
her hand stitched the perfecting dart
in bridal satin. She brought report
of cars arriving, clear skies
towards the church. They were her tears
(pew-stifled) from which the happiest
laughter billowed confetti outside the church doors.
Of best wishes, loudest were hers.

And nobody thanked her. Why doesn't
she mind her own business? they said—
who'd leant upon her. Crude and peasant-like
her interest in brides and the dead.
I thought so too, yet still was loath

to add my voice, sensing that
my secret poems were like her actions: both
pried into love and savoured death.

St. Mark's, Cheetham Hill

Designed to dominate the district—
God being nothing if not large
and stern, melancholic from man's fall
(like Victoria widowed early)—
the church, its yard, were raised on a plateau
six feet above the surrounding green.
There weren't many houses then; Manchester
was a good walk away. I've seen
faded photographs: the church standing
amid strolling gentry, as though
ready to sail for the Empire's farthest parts—
the Union Jack at the tower's masthead
enough to quell upstart foreigners and natives.
But those were the early days. The city
began to gollop profits, burst
outward on all sides. Soon,
miles of the cheapest brick swaddled landmarks—
the church one. Chimes, that had used to wake
workers in Whitefield, died in near streets.

From our house (a part of the parish)
St. Mark's is a turn right, a turn left,
and straight down Coke Street past the "Horseshoe."
The raised graveyard—full these many years—
overlooks the junction of five streets:
pollarded plane trees round its edge,
the railings gone to help fight Hitler.
Adam Murray of New Galloway,
"Who much improved the spinning mule,"
needs but a step from his tomb to peer in
at somebody's glittering television.
Harriet Pratt, "A native of Derby,"
might sate her judgement-hunger with chips

were she to rise and walk twenty yards.
The houses are that close. The church,
begrimed, an ugly irregular box
squatting above those who once filled it
with faith and praise, looks smaller now
than in those old pictures. Subdued
by a raincoat factory's bulk, the Kosher
Slaughter House next door, its dignity
is rare weddings, the Co-op hearse,
and hired cars full of elderly mourners.

The congregations are tiny nowadays,
few folk could tell you whether it's "High" or "Low."
The vicar's name, the times of services,
is specialized knowledge. And fear has gone:
the damp, psalmed, God of my childhood has gone.
Perhaps a boy delivering papers
in winter darkness before the birds awake
keeps to Chapel Street's far side, for fear
some corpse interred at his ankle's depth
might shove a hand through the crumbling wall
and grab him in passing; but not for fear
of black religion—the blurred bulk
of God in drizzle and dirty mist,
or hooded with snow on his white throne
watching the sparrow fall.
                                    Now, the graveyard—
its elegant wrought-ironwork wrenched,
carted away; its rhymed epitaphs,
urns of stone and ingenious scrolls
chipped, tumbled, masked by weeds—
is used as a playground. Shouting children
Tiggy between the tombs.
                                    On Saturdays
I walk there sometimes—through the drift
of jazz from open doors, the tide
of frying fish, and the groups of women

gossiping on their brushes—to see the church,
its God decamped, or dead, or daft
to all but the shrill hosannas of children
whose prayers are laughter, playing such parts
in rowdy games you'd think it built
for no greater purpose, think its past
one long term of imprisonment.

Little survives Authority's cant
but the forgotten, the written-off,
and the misunderstood. The Methodist chapel's
been bought by the Jews for a synagogue;
Ukrainian Catholics have the Wesleyan's
sturdy structure built to outlast Rome—
and men of the district say St. Mark's
is part of a clearance area. Soon
it will be down as low as rubble
from every house that squeezed it round,
to bed a motorway and a new estate.
Or worse: repainted, pointed, primmed—
as becomes a unit in town-planners'
clever dreams of a healthy community—
will prosper in dignity and difference,
the gardened centre of new horizons.

Rather than this I'd see a ruin,
and picture the final splendours of decay:
Opposing gangs in wild "Relievo,"
rushing down aisles and dusty pews
at which the houses look straight in
past broken wall; and late-night drunkards
stumbling their usual short-cut home
across uneven eulogies, fumbling
difficult flies to pour discomfort out
in comfortable shadows, in a nave
they praise with founts, and moonlit blooms of steam.

Elegy for Alfred Hubbard

Hubbard is dead, the old plumber:
who will mend our burst pipes now,
the tap that has dripped all the summer,
testing the sink's overflow?

No other like him. Young men with knowledge
of new techniques and theories from books
may better his work, straight from college,
but who will challenge his squint-eyed looks

in kitchen, bathroom, under floorboards,
rules of thumb which were often wrong;
seek as erringly stopcocks in cupboards,
or make a job last half as long?

He was a man who knew the ginnels,
alleyways, streets—the whole district:
family secrets, minor annals,
time-honoured fictions fused to fact.

Seventy years of gossip muttered
under his cap, his tufty thatch,
so that his talk was slow and clotted,
hard to follow, and too much.

As though nothing fell, none vanished,
and time were the maze of Cheetham Hill,
in which the dead—with jobs unfinished—
waited to hear him ring the bell.

For much he never got round to doing,
but meant to, when weather bucked up,

or worsened, or when his pipe was drawing,
or when he'd finished this cup.

I thought time, he forgot so often,
had forgotten him; but here's Death's pomp
over his house, and by the coffin
the son who will inherit his blowlamp,

tools, workshop, cart, and cornet
(pride of Cheetham Prize Brass Band),
and there's his mourning widow, Janet,
stood at the gate he'd promised to mend.

Soon he will make his final journey:
shaved and silent, strangely trim,
with never a pause to talk to any-
body: how arrow-like, for him!

In St. Mark's Church, whose dismal tower
he pointed and painted when a lad,
they will sing his praises amidst flowers
while, somewhere, a cellar starts to flood,

and the housewife banging his front-door knocker
is not surprised to find him gone,
and runs for Thwaite, who's a better worker,
and sticks at a job until it's done.

Apologue

Having a fine new suit,
and no invitations,
I slept in my new suit
hoping to induce
a dream of fair women.

And did indeed: the whole night long,
implored by naked
beauty—pink on white linen—
I struggled to remove
my fine new suit.

At dawn I awoke, blear-eyed,
sweating beneath encumbering rags.

Community Singing

Grandad Connor toiled at the forge
may his bones dance his bones sing,
his heart was shrunk but his lust large,
he tricked at cards and worshipped God
kept his wife in perennial pod
butter he ate and the rest marge,
a straight street and nothing in sight.

Uncle Henry trained as a clerk
may his bones dance his bones sing,
to sit on his arse was too much like work,
one morning he stayed steady in bed
and lay supine till the day he died,
some men won't leave a thing to luck,
a straight street and nothing in sight.

This was our Jack, and Auntie Prue
may their bones dance their bones sing,
both had serious tasks to do
Jack went daft with a hell of a fuss
and Prue fell under a fifty-five bus,
the family grave excused the two,
a straight street and nothing in sight.

Cousin Arthur followed the dogs
may his bones dance his bones sing,
natty his bow and Oxford Bags
cute the monogram on his shirts
oh what a hit with the classy skirts,
struck down on a night of jig-a-jigs,
a straight street and nothing in sight.

Dad was a lad with a golden tongue
may his bones dance his bones sing,
went overboard at the sirens' song,
left his heart on a butcher's slab
swopped his beads for a pack of tabs
said he wouldn't be gone long,
a straight street and nothing in sight.

Here's a prayer for all the lot,
may their bones dance their bones sing.
The blossom must fall to form the fruit,
Troy was sacked for a third-rate verse
a woman's pout and a toy horse.
Torn-up Orpheus twang that lute,
a straight street and nothing in sight.

October in Clowes Park

The day dispossessed of light. At four o'clock
in the afternoon, a sulphurous, manufactured
twilight, smudging the scummed lake's far side,
leant on the park. Sounds, muffled—
as if the lolling muck clogged them at the source—
crawled to the ear. A skyed ball thudded
to ground, a swan leathered its wings by the island.
I stood and watched a water-hen arrow
shutting silver across the sooty mat
of the lake's surface—an earl's lake,
though these fifty years the corporation's.
And what is left of the extensive estate
(a few acres of scruffy, flat land
framing this wet sore in the minds of property agents)
a public park. All else is built on.
Through swags of trees poked the bare backsides
of encircling villas, gardening-sheds:
a ring of light making the park dimmer.
Boys and men shouldering long rods—
all licensed fishers, by their open way—
scuffled the cinders past me, heading for home;
but I stayed on—the dispossessed day
held me, turned me towards the ruined Hall.
Pulsing in that yellow, luminous, murk
(a trick of the eye), the bits of broken pillar
built into banks, the last upright wall,
the stalactite-hung split shells of stables,
seemed likely to find a voice—such pent-in grief
and anger!—or perhaps to explode silently
with force greater than any known to progress,
wiping the district, town, kingdom, age,
to darkness far deeper than that which fluffed

now at the neat new urinal's outline,
and heaved and beat behind it in the ruins.
Like a thud in the head, suddenly become memory,
stillness was dumb around me. Scrambling up
a heap of refuse I grabbed at crystalled brick.
Flakes fell from my hand—a gruff tinkle—
no knowledge there of what brought the Hall low,
or concern either. Neither did I care.
Irrecoverably dead, slumped in rank weed
and billowy grass, it mouldered from here to now,
connoting nothing but where my anger stood
and grief enough to pull the sagging smoke
down from the sky, a silent, lethal, swaddling
over the garden I played in as a child,
and over those children—laughter in the branches—
shaking the pear-tree's last sour fruit to ground.

An Empty House

Doors bolted; windows dirt-bleared.
Was ever invitation sent
to cross this garden, vilely littered
with ashes, garbage, once-elegant

columned Olympians;—toppled, broken?
No; but rabid ignoramus,
feckless far-from-home, wise man
exceeding wisdom, and various

frustrated ghosts, hover, strut,
slouch, and scribble in these grounds.
Forgotten squatters, from mere habit
raising occasional, imploring, hands

in antic faith. A common blindness
fudges with wishes dead hope;
the towers are fallen that were topless;
nothing left but strife, wrought shape!

Some few, compelled by pride to seek
the truth, scream, curse, take poison,
weep until their hearts break,
peering on cobwebs, splendour gone.

The best, sad-eyed, quick with courage,
admit an ending. Gather, dustbin
their old love-letters, damp from the garage,
and leave to work, to father children.

The Burglary

It's two o'clock now; somebody's pausing in the street
to turn up his collar. The night's black: distraught
with chimney-toppling wind and harsh rain—
see, the wet's soaking in on the end-gable,
and the frothing torrent, overspilling the broken drain,

accosts the pavement with incoherent babble.
There is the house we want: how easy to burgle,
with its dark trees, and the lawn set back from the road.
The owners will be in bed now—the old couple;
you've got the position of the safe?—Yes, I know the code.

The cock's going mad up there on the church steeple,
the wind's enormous—will it ever stifle;
still, its noise and the rain's are with us, I daresay:
they'll cover what we make, if we go careful
round by the greenhouse and in at the back way.

Here's the broken sash I mentioned—no need to be fearful.
Watch how I do it, these fingers are facile
with the practice I've had on worse nights than this.
I tell you, the whole thing's going to be a doddle:
the way I've got it worked out, we can't miss.

Although, God knows, most things turn out a muddle,
and it only confuses more to look for a moral.
Wherever I've been the wind and the rain's blown—
I've done my best to hang on as they tried to whittle
the name from the action, the flesh away from the bone,

but I think, sometimes, I'm fighting a losing battle.
So many bad nights, so many strange homes to burgle,

and every job done with a mate I don't know—
oh, you're all right: I don't mean to be personal,
but when the day breaks you'll have your orders, and go.

Then the next time the foul weather howls in the ginnel,
when the slates slide, the brimming gutters gurgle,
there'll be another lad I've never seen before,
with the rest of the knowledge that makes the job possible
as I ease up a window or skeleton-key a door.

Still, it's my only life, and I've no quarrel
with the boss's methods—apart from the odd quibble
about allowances and fair rates of pay,
or the difficult routes I often have to travel,
or the fact that I never get a holiday.

Most of the time, though, I'm glad of mere survival,
even at the stormiest hour of the darkest vigil.
. . . Here's the hall door; under the stairs, you said?
This one's easy because the old folk are feeble,
and lie in their curtained room sleeping like the dead.

Sometimes, believe me, it's a lot more trouble,
when you've got to be silent, and move as though through
        treacle.
Now hold your breath while I let these tumblers click . . .
I've done these many a time . . . a well-known model . . .
one more turn now . . . Yes, that does the trick.

Nothing inside? The same recurrent muddle!
I think the most careful plan's a bloody marvel
if it plays you true, if nothing at all goes wrong.
Well, let's be off. We've another place to tackle
under the blown black rain, and the dawn won't be long

when the wind will drop and the rain become a drizzle,
and you'll go your way. Leaving me the bedraggled

remnants of night, that walk within the head
long after the sun-shot gutters cease to trickle,
and I draw my curtains and topple into bed.

Porto Venere

One midnight, glittering-eyed, in restless silence,
she left our bed, the tower where we were lodged,
and hurried to the sea. The moon was full.
Over the lanterns in the square, the dancing
couples who'd stay till dawn, it swung seaward
through legions of tiny clouds; and she—high-breasted
beside the harbour's fidget of clunking boats—
blanched and burrowed among the shifting shadows,
hearing only the lonely grotto's roar—
like the moon's voice, or the voice of her own blood.

I did not see her go, but dozed heavy
with wine under the wounds of a pallid icon,
and dreamed her body clung so close to mine
spindrift of sweat scattered from huge surges
of muscled battering, undertow sucked back
surfacing faces, thrust, and filled, and killed
everything but the sea's—until she lay
salty and heavy-eyed within my arms,
murmuring: "Love, the waves, the waves were awful.
The moon went in. I thought that I might drown."

In Autumn, begin.
              Uprooting geraniums,
shaking them gently for storage in darkness,
had heard guns crackle in far streets.
In the deepening sky, one evening,
a plane wrote "Freedom"—a vaporous trail
gone before sunset.
              Beyond the city, mountains—
most often hidden. On clear days certain fields,
a pike, glinting glass. Many went that way,
wheels rumbling towards rock.
                     None saw a good end.
The last birds flew late. South, eagerly
when they went. Still, sparrows at my door
importuned for what bread?

Guard against draughts. Bolt the banging door.

Sat late by small oil, a moth, and one moment's silence.
Books helped me, so did other things:
crossword puzzles, meditation.
                 November rain
stained the chimney breast,
at night the wounded groaned beyond the hedge.
The sink froze.
             All day long the tanks clattered past,
disturbing earth, churning up cobbles.
Not a face I knew. Guns pointing onwards.

Christmas is nothing without a child.

Ghosts again in the front room.
I thought they'd gone for good, but meaning no harm.

Seeking their own echoes, I think.
Their faces in mirrors.
                              And then . . .
New men with the first green shoots.
Declarations, manifestoes, promises
in shoddy eccentric type on grey paper.
"There will be public trials . . .
                              full restitution . . ."
Dreamed often: four friends dead,
one in exile, one a traitor to some cause.
But could not say the rest.
After the big winds the battle came back;
                              muddled,
beyond the understanding of many.
The snipers stayed longest,
                              and the sky brightened,
imperceptibly, towards summer.
Twigs from laburnum cluttered the front path.
One branch snapped abruptly while I watched,
suggesting more death.

Sharpen the good saw.

Noticed willowherb in unlikely places:
on the roofs of outside privies, in formal gardens.
Dock leaf and dandelion brightened the ruins
beyond my care.
                    The cat went out, never came back,
but the strawberries ripened well. This gave pleasure.
In the topmost room the lodger, enfeebled,
scrabbled the quilt, called for a priest,
                              or rabbi.
Only a lay preacher came, and he starved and rambling.

Trim the hedge. Sweep the cellar. Send letters.

One day it was over, or seemed to be.
                              Someone said
a van with a loudspeaker telling good news . . .
I think someone said that. And near the end
the birds came back, or perhaps they just came out
to see August, with the din of brass-bands,
flaunting banners, throwing down arms in the street.
How the children shouted!
                              How the women cried!
I smiled in the garden, clutching a dead root,
and the thrush stood on the aerial opposite,
singing! singing!
                  Old friends returned,
drank my new wine.
                  I welcomed them home.

25

In Oak Terrace

Old and alone, she sits at nights
nodding before the television.
The house is quiet now. She knits,
rises to put the kettle on,

watches a cowboy's killing, reads
the local Births and Deaths, and falls
asleep at "Growing stock-piles of war-heads."
A world that threatens worse ills

fades. She dreams of a life spent
in the one house: suffers again
poverty, sickness, abandonment,
a child's death, a brother's brain

melting to madness. Seventy years
of common trouble; the kettle sings.
At midnight she says her silly prayers,
and takes her teeth out, and collects her night-things.

Mayor Isaac Watts

Beyond my great-grandfather's bulk
of waistcoat, beard, and arrogant head,
riddle the dumb couplings it took
to raise him up, to fix his blood.

Firm, on a blanched photograph,
face set as though against light's
attrition, he is the last rough
signpost before the track fades out.

The family seeks no farther back:
issued from God Gloucester gentry
is pride-favoured. This is a rock
worth many a longer history

of shifting fortunes. Only mine
the thoughts that pierce the foxy dark
caught in his eyes: that won't have done
until the dubious dead awake

clamouring at his shoulders. Tramp,
didicoy, son and son conceived
at village fête or harvest romp,
the pretty maid the bailiff loved,

until she swelled—let them appear:
fathers who drank winter away,
families that fought tooth and claw,
graceless lumps of Cotswold clay.

Kneaded together, wrenched apart
I'll see them dance: a toppling rote

of clumsy figures, gay and hurt,
then rammed home down death's throat.

For surer than recollected pride,
known quantities, titles that limn
the civil, virtuous and well-shod,
this rabble makes the man I am

labour at poems, seeking in words
a crude power, anonymous
as all the unnumbered heads
that haunt my great-grandfather's eyes.

A Woman Dying

In a room with a wardrobe far too large—
bought at a sale cheap, or handed down—
this careless woman struggled for breath.
Faded oilcloth stopped short of the skirting boards;
beneath her pyjama-top there flowered
the vivid, cancerous sores. She lay with death.

Chrysanthemums in a white bowl
held their tongues, were not telling the name
of whoever had brought them. Now and then
neighbours and friends appeared to be by her side.
Her husband came, spoke, went—so did the pain;
nightdark, daylight, nightdark, and daylight again.

Already nothingness hung like a smell
among the factual furniture. The bare
bulb in its rusty socket rocked
substance away as her younger sister slept.
"Is that burglars?" she said in the small hours,
who had never worried whether the door was locked.

Something was different, something had come in
through fifty-six years of doors left on the latch,
that fed on neglected duties: dust
gathering unswept, meals she'd forgotten to make.
Perhaps it would go if she did her best:
on tiny observances she fretted dully and fussed.

But could not make redress, nor pay
attention enough to keep her sister's face
sharp as her memory of it. Trees
beyond the window waved branches of goodbye,

and then: "What was it the branches waved?"
Question and answer were like as two peas.

And neither mattered. The pain blanked out
everything but a lusting after death,
or youth, or sleep—they looked the same.
Whatever knew friendly flesh was good, was God.
She choked and spat and coughed and tore
down Heaven with moans until the doctor came

A needle eased the world away.
She did not see the window's curdled shine
grow fronds and flowers which multiplied
all night despite that thrusting, fiery, breath.
At dawn winter went on without her,
while by the bed her sister stood and cried.

Waking

The incubus of nightmare is on my chest
squeezing the rib-cage in. What beast
squats on its haunches, face to mine,
waiting for me to wake, and open
eyes like an owl's—so close are his?
I lie sweating eternities
of clouded fears away until,
hearing the milkman ring the bell,
I know the customary world awaits
beyond my darkness. The incubus fits
a sticky finger into my nose
to find out where the nostril goes.
It is my eldest son—no worse—
two years commander of this universe:
an incubus which babbles "Daddy"
over the pouchy, ageing body
which surely should be small as his
is small, and should be racing downstairs
to the kitchen fire, and a huge man
who laughs and laughs and says "Hello, son."

An Evening at Home

Sensing a poem about to happen,
two letters demanded to be written.

One to a man about a dog
began clearly and ended vaguely;

the other, to a girl for old times' sake,
overstepped the bounds of propriety. My teeth began to ache.

From a single suspect raw-edged tooth
the pain spread all over my mouth

before I could stop it. Coupled with
rising flatulence, it nearly overcame faith

in my sacred calling. But back I fought
with a concentration of poetic thought

upon my desk. I almost went over
from the chair in which I'd sat to recover—

and would have done had not the lodger knocked
to say that his sink waste-pipe was blocked.

Using the plunger, I began to feel jaded
and disillusioned: something more was needed

than mere poems to right the world.
My hands were numb, I remembered the millions killed

in God's name. I remembered bombs, gas-chambers, famine,
        poverty,
and my greying hair. I could not write poetry.

My nose tingled as though it was going to bleed.
I shut my notebook quietly and went to bed.

The Smell

The smell hangs about the bedroom,
and can't be got rid of. Open door
and window, the smell will disappear
for a half-hour, then back it comes

as strong as ever. I don't like
it: part of it's me, mixed with powders,
perfumes, lotions, and hair-lacquers
from that loaded dressing-table of hers.

My smell used to be mine: a treat
to savour in a single bed,
a secret with God. Now my sweat,
sex and gases have been compounded

into a woman's property. Now
my smell is something she wears when
she strips herself for love. I
fear it will not be mine again.

A Death in the Family

My father died
the spring I was twenty-five. It had been
a dragging winter. The night was cold
when a distant cousin of his we'd never seen
knocked at the door to tell us. We smiled
uncertainly at one another.
Nobody cried,

none of us grieved—
why should we? He'd been absent for too long:
even my mother couldn't find a tear
to mourn him with. She'd grown strong,
hardened against him in the twenty years
since the day he'd gone, saying he'd be back—
and she'd believed

he would be back.
My sister and I couldn't remember
much about him, and what we could
might have been false. I thought I'd clambered
towards his smile on a rumpled bed,
she felt in her hand a shilling he'd given her, but the tales
made us lose track—

tales we'd been told.
We didn't know what was ours or hearsay
so many people he'd called his friends
had stayed around us, whose every memory or stray
comment fed our starved minds.
But we never thought of his coming back,
or growing old.

"Ironic," I said
to my mother that cold spring night—
the visitor gone, ourselves at table—
"That a man can pass from all knowledge and sight
of family for twenty years. Can dissemble
completely, and yet be found-out
as soon as dead."

This is the way
we'd talked of him always, as though he were
a case in the papers. Not, I think,
to put him in perspective, but to ensure
that neither self-pity nor the rank
tendrils of guilt choked the life of the household.
Day by day

he receded farther
into the regions of myth—to which,
no doubt, he'd banished us. Images
do not hurt as much as people; such
details as we gathered were appendices
to empty pages. Our only
parent was a mother.

But we were wrong,
my sister and I,—my mother as well:
calling him "John Connor," with no
suggestion she'd ever slept with him at all.
It took his death to rescue him from limbo:
to give again to an abstract evil
a human tongue.

My Father's Walking-Stick

Swindler, con-man, and embezzler
are a few of the roles my father played.
Declared a bankrupt in '32,
he opened a radio shop in my mother's name,
forging her signature to save time and trouble.
She was the only daughter among
a pack of lads—the last at home,
when he met her. She and a widowed mother
in a well-kept house. No wonder his lodger's eye
brightened towards the ageing girl.
Soon my grandma was baking him meat pies,
calling him "Son."
                    It must have seemed
a good arrangement to all concerned: he,
with the urge to procreate that visits
philandering men after years of contraceptives—
but no home-making instinct, found
a home already made; my mother,
fiercely dutiful, thought she could add
a husband to what existed; my grandma
imagined daughter and self provided for.
Perhaps there was love, too. I can't
answer for that—although my mother
even at sixty-nine's a sucker for silver-tongued men.

Snapshots show him in a cap
with a big neb, his arm round her
on a boat to the Isle of Man: both
are smiling three months before my birth.
Later there's one of her in a laughing pose
next to the backyard dustbin. Taken
by him, it looks affectionate—as though

he'd said, as he clicked the shutter: "Let's
have it backwards-road-about tonight."

But my mother's fervent, legal, honesty
must have shocked him. Out of bed
he couldn't persuade her to accept
his improvisations. When angry creditors
and detectives called, she jibbed at saying:
"I'm sorry, he's gone to London on business."
According to their different lights
they let each other down badly. I was five
when he disappeared with a Royal Warrant
out for his arrest. None of us saw
him again, but twenty years on,
incredibly breaking silence, came news
of his distant death.

                    Among his belongings
(the woman he'd lived with had them in a cardboard
grocery box ready for me to claim or reject)
I found a stout walking-stick.
Thinking it apt that, having been
without support from him for so long,
my mother should have something of him
to lean on at last, I carried it home
three hundred miles under my arm.
Her comment was flat, but had an edge
I couldn't name: "Put it in the hall-stand."
There it has stood, unused, to this day.

My Mother's Husband

My mother worries more
as she grows old, about that period
when he was at home. Not that she ever
admits to doubt of her ramrod-
straight honesty's perfect right
to feel outraged at his behaviour,
not that she says there was some wrong
on her side too—no matter how little.
The way her mind turns back
is like a child retracing steps on a dark night,
vainly scrabbling ground for the bright
coin it had gone to purchase sweets with—
unable, even, to find the hole
through which it must have slipped.

Sometimes she makes a joke
of how her conscience settled
all the bills he let go hang
when he disappeared, or of her luck
in picking such a fool
of a man from all the ones she kept
dangling from her little finger.
More often, though, she sees his criminal streak
as author of her tragedy,
unfailingly lumping with it, even now
not daring to consider longer—
his cruel trick
of being different: deliberately
taking the other side, the opposite view
from "everyone else." I think of my
serious clashes with her rigid mind:
her closings, with a blind
"You're getting like your father."

At seventy there are certain new
infinitesimal hints of tone-
changes in the iron mockery
with which she tells of how he'd go
miles to hear a thing called "Lohengrin,"
and how she's seen him, thick with lather—
foaming from ear to ear—
posturing at the mirror like a loon,
reciting soliloquies by Shakespeare.

A Death by the Seaside

1

Too clearly for my comfort, I am able
to picture a likely ending for myself;
not slain by Gods, or torn apart by rabble,
or making a last insanely proud and wilful
stand against storm or sea, but rather, a quiet
lodger—the only guest—in a boarding house
where stairs are being moved, walls knocked out,
and the downstairs parlour changed to a cocktail lounge
ready for next season. A man of sixty,
or thereabouts, who writes no letters. At night,
a man who sits alone, staring fixedly
at each successive programme on the bright
screen amidst the contractor's half-completed
contemporary fittings. Type of Timon—
but not disgusted enough to be great—
I see myself, a soured old man—a "rum 'un"
to landlady and cleaners; one whose ways,
and presence by the shore in dead of winter
are cause for speculation "though he pays
on the dot each Friday." One who has no banter,
and little luggage, who walks the gusty prom
sick of the past, impatient for death to come.

2

I'm thinking of my father, and the stroke
that finished him off a long long way from home.
He was a man who gorged till he was sick:
wife, children, friends, desire, Rome—

he rid himself of the lot. Moderate men
take nourishment from a diet such as this;
he was immoderate, always. He moved on,
revolted by his vomit. The curdled mess

looked nothing like the tasty meal he'd eaten—
it ruined his appetite. The very sight
of others' relish turned his soul. The glutton
became ascetic: he ate hardly a bite

for twenty years, and died nowty and cold,
uncared for and uncaring. In his room
a youthful policeman riffled through the old
thrillers and cowboy stories after him.

3

My teeth are good, my vision's twenty-twenty,
my flesh attracts the women that I want;
at thirty-four I am a horn of plenty,
a prodigal with riches. From this point

in time, I could believe the past a gift:
accumulated selves (not one that's dead,
redundant, or drags-on crippled)—hefty
schoolboys and soldiers performing in my head

the instant's deeds; but when I cut my finger
flesh gathers slowly like a ripening pod,
straining to close the fissure, 'flu takes longer
to clear, I wake in the small hours, afraid

my sons are Cain and Abel. Worse, I see
my face—that untamed creature—taking the look
of my father's in old snaps. Age is drawing me
towards him: I might repeat his mistake,

am capable of doing. Why must I mount my wife
so often her flesh cloys? Why must I play games
with the children till they irritate and bore me, love
God so fiercely that I needs must deny his claims?

4

I'll exercise for extinction on a beach
empty except for some old cripple's dog,
that's left its master dangling a slipped leash
and trying to whistle. The face of Woolworths' clock—
handless, as though time itself departed
on the tail of the crowds—will help prepare me for
the nothingness to come. I'll visit martyred
heroes, and film stars, rapists, churchmen, whores,
in Madame Tussaud's; then (when I hear my blood
rumouring death's arrival) winter's fallen
Babylon of the Pleasure Park. My mood,
confirming its valedictory lack of all
regret, will fasten on the apparatus
for easing profit from the nation's fools:
the River Caves' smeared plaster, the ramshackle phallus
of Jack and Jill, the body-stinking vault
of the Fun House. And there I'll make my will,
in front of the clockwork clown whose collapsed hulk
skulks behind shutters, leering, silent, still:
"Fuck-all for anyone." He will witness me
before I shuffle back to die alone,
shrieking for human aid.
                                    Next summer he
will shriek without one added overtone.

The Poet's District

My mind runs on and back and round:
routes of my childhood fixed the shape
of thought; I cannot now escape
shadowy entries, streets that wind,
alleys that are often blind.

The games I played on winter nights—
chancing a labyrinth of dark
limbos between the gaslamps—mark
me one who races fears and doubts
with bated breath, whose short cuts

are tumbling trespasses through sad
gardens abandoned by the rich,
whose hints to pursuers, roughly scratched
arrows on brick and cryptic words
only with difficulty deciphered.

Bounded by solitude, and walls,
and brews that peter out on crofts,
concealed corners, sudden shifts
of level, backs that flirt with ginnels,
double round privies, skirt schools—

deviously beneath the close
horizons of houses, through streets
grown nightmare-still, I take thought
towards that final hiding place
where someone crouches with my face

waiting impatient to be found
and freed by a swift, relieving tig.

I am small and fearful. Very big
and quiet, and cold, and unconcerned,
the tricky district of my mind.

The Graveyard

One winter morning, half in a dream,
the young boy lurched from his heaped bed
before the sky hinted at light.
The window, encrusted with frosty flowers,
concealed the tangle of whispering streets
knotted together around the graveyard.

All night long he had dreamed of the graveyard,
and now he recalled it was more than a dream:
it waited for him among the streets.
Oh how he wished to be warm in bed!
He rubbed a hole in the frosty flowers,
saw cold darkness, and switched on the light.

He hated to be out before it was light
delivering papers; and though the graveyard—
its waiting tombs and cobweb flowers—
was what disturbed him and made him dream,
he wouldn't have got from the lumpiest bed
to walk the pleasantest dawn-wet streets

given the choice. And yet the streets
were where he must go. In the acrid light
of the bare bulb he dressed by the bed,
shivering with cold and thoughts of the graveyard.
He tried to forget his horrible dream
of a hand beckoning from grey grave-flowers.

He wished he delivered bread, or flowers—
jobs of the cheerful, daytime streets—
but how could he, at eleven, dream
of saying: "I'll only work when it's light?"

His mother laughed when he spoke of the graveyard;
she said: "It's just that you like your bed!"

He laced his boots and made his bed,
straightening the quilt's misshapen flowers,
and soon he was on his way to the graveyard
by a rambling route that led through streets
dark between pools of feeble gaslight.
He delivered his papers as though in a dream.

It was faintly light when he reached the graveyard.
The streets whispered: "Have you brought flowers
for the dead who dream of you in their narrow beds?"

Lodgers

They came with somewhere else in view,
but scrambled to retrieve my ball,
and smiled and told me tales. I grew
within their shadows: Chew, and Nall,
Entwistle, Mounsor, Mitcham, Grey—
masterful men who could not stay.

Some boozed and came in late, and some
kept to their bedrooms every night,
some liked a joke, and some were glum,
and all of them were always right.
Unwitting fathers; how their deep
voices come back to me in sleep!

I hear them mumbling through the wall
nursery prayers and drunken smut.
I see their hairy fingers maul
sandwiches delicately cut.
I smell their smoky suits, their sweat,
salute them all, and own my debt.

They came, they fidgeted, they went.
Able to settle nowhere long,
theirs were the terms of banishment
that clothe the skeleton. Their strong
fathering figures could afford
little beyond their bed and board.

And yet: enough. Each exile's mite
of manhood—noble in its fall—
bestowed upon me helped me write

a name on nothing. Chew, and Nall,
Entwistle, Mounsor, Mitcham, Grey—
masterful men who could not stay.

The Small Hours in the Kitchen

Last night in sweltering heat at one o'clock
I worked again, with no one else awake.

Behind my naked back as I crouched tense
by a yellow door unmarked as innocence,

I felt the house—its corridors and rooms—
seething invisibly with my family's dreams,

as though it were a sea I dare not look back on,
deep, dark, and featureless to an horizon

unimaginably distant, and I, near-drowned,
stretching from shallows towards unknown land.

I watched my arm extending and the latch
become a shining black-enamelled patch

under my brush. I saw, almost within
my eyeballs, then as tics on the air's skin,

the million moving motes of sand-papered dust
breath raised from the floor. I smelled the waste

clogging the sewers beneath the roads that led
from me to everywhere. I walked my own head

among the sleeping race huddled in fear
in innumerable beds. I saw the same sleeper

smoking quietly in caverns underground
waiting by panelled dials for the last command

from the same sleeper treading a different dream
of noble lives made barbarous by decision.

The heat had brought a sweat out on my brow.
Making its landing run a jet came low

over the house. At quarter past one o'clock
I saw its fairy lights, and its shape, black

against flocks of cloud. I heard the refrigerator
begin to freeze again—a sullen whirr

that ate the buzz in my skull. Upon the door
I saw a mark I had not seen before.

Entering the City

The city lies ahead. The vale
is cluttering as the train speeds through.
Hacked woods fall back. The scoop and swell
of cooling towers swing into view.

Acres of clinker, slag-heaps, roads
where lorries rev and tip all night,
railway sidings, broken sheds
brutally bare in arc-light,

summon me to a present far
from Pericles's Athens, Caesar's Rome,
to follow again the river's scar
squirming beneath detergent foam.

I close my book, and rub the glass:
a glance ambiguously dark
entertains briefly scrap-yards, rows
of houses, and a treeless park,

like passing thoughts. Across my head
sundry familiar and strange
denizens of the city tread
vistas I would, and would not, change.

Birth-place and home! The diesel's whine
flattens. Excited and defiled
once more, I heave the window down
and thrust my head out like a child.

Lancashire Winter

The town remembers no such plenty,
under the wind from off the moor.
The labour exchange is nearly empty;
stiletto heels on the Palais floor
move between points of patent leather.
Sheepskin coats keep out the weather.

Commerce and Further Education
won't be frozen. Dully free
in snack bars and classrooms sits the patient
centrally heated peasantry,
receiving Wimpies like the Host;
striving to get That Better Post.

Snow on the streets and Mini-Minors
thickens to drifts, and in the square
from dingy plinths, blind eyes, stone collars,
the fathers of revolution stare,
who—against pikes and burning brands—
built the future with bare hands.

Old Beswick

Always death's companion—bearded,
stooping to earth and mumble-worded
with flower heads, dug-up roots, the hutched
rabbits he fed on crisp lettuce and grass fetched
each day fresh from his nursery garden—
he was the terror of my childhood. Forbidden
things lurked in the steam behind his patched
greenhouse glass; both his legs were wooden.

It took years of my growing-up
to cleanse from sleep the bedraggled gap
in a hedge through which, with a mouthful of curses,
he came at me once, his pee-stained baggy trousers
slapping those rigid limbs. A lad
told me all of him was turning into wood—
his own coffin, the kids whispered. Houses
were safe and so were streets: I stayed in and read,

and played amidst the comfort of alleys,
blotting his holy of black holies
out of my mind with hopscotch, tig,
Masterman Ready, errands with basket or jug,
and homework. Never daring to trespass
again in that part of the park where an ivied buttress
leant on the Hall's remaining wall—a sag
and stagger of crystalled brick bounding the monstrous

garden where he, flowers, steam,
rabbits, and death, kept bloodstopping company. Time
plays strange tricks on memory: he married
a young widow, when I was twenty and hadn't worried
or dreamed about him for years. His face,

elderly and benign, smiled from the close
print of the local paper, but my sleep was harried
anew by the old evil, roaring its curse

on all imposture, the open furnaces
of its eyes dazzling the lake, and the houses
beyond the gates, as I ran and ran
away through the years, and on on on
came the wooden legs, lurching the fiery
twilight at every step, till the mouth hairy
and vast as God's cried, "Perish the man
that takes my name in vain," and I woke in a fury

of sweat and sheets, sure that death
for the old man had burst from the pith
of a child's nightmare into the present,
and through the dawn-wet streets hastened
that moment towards his marriage bed.
He lived for years longer. People said,
when he died, that but for arthritic hips there wasn't
a thing wrong with him: what an end for a good

old soul—to slip and fall in the nursery
garden he'd made his life! Wary
of whatever was to disturb, I kept
away for ages. Then, on a day nipped
by autumn's first teeth, returning
from somewhere beyond the park, I smelled leaves burning,
and trod again the familiar path between lopped
columns, fallen corbels, and ironwork turning

wholly to rust in bushy grass.
Silence. And woodsmoke curling across
a waste of weeds. In seeding cabbage
the hutches were random planks. A heap of garbage
rotted amongst the broken pipes

of the caved greenhouse. I wondered what hopes
proved false, as I walked—devoid of fear or courage—
towards the young keeper's fire by the small copse.

A Child Half-Asleep

Stealthily parting the small-hours silence,
a hardly-embodied figment of his brain
comes down to sit with me
as I work late.
Flat-footed, as though his legs and feet
were still asleep.

He sits on a stool,
staring into the fire,
his dummy dangling.

Fire ignites the small coals of his eyes.
It stares back through the holes
into his head, into the darkness.

I ask what woke him?

"A wolf dreamed me" he says.

Considering Junk

It lies there, vivid in its dereliction,
among fine ashes from combustion stoves,
drippings of tinned tomatoes
that smelled peculiar, soiled disposable
nappies, and other household grot.

Having exhausted, or frustrated expectation,
it emanates a certain smugness—
if you are of such a mind to think so.

A painter might take away the slither
of red polythene down a scorched bucket
into the crumbly texture of old flock
beneath, a sculptor (to the point of plundering)
broken bannister-ends like totems
to an ultimate, perfect, mass beyond masses.

You may look at it in different ways . . .

There are, for instance, certainly, numerous
homilies here for the religious man
with a touch of the poet.
                              As for the poet
himself: in this rigorous age he is wary of metaphor,
far more of symbol, and if he is the householder
(as I am) whose annual clear-out
has overflowed dustbin, grocery-boxes,
and mildewed split trunk, onto
the garden path, his dreams alone are likely
to dwell on things he threw away.
                              Cumbersome, brokendown
junk talking all night with the eloquence of poems.

Saying It

Questions of tact are uppermost,
even when control appears to be lost.
To develop which, one cultivates silence
as well as words, weighing to the ounce
pauses long and short, awkward searchings,
and constructions that chase themselves in rings
till they peter away in utter defeat.
There may be a notable tact in that.
As in giving an embarrassing amount away,
in "baring the soul" autobiographically,
in being tactless. What is demanded
is that the poet be openhanded
enough to allow his skill to grip
of all possible shapes the one shape
without which the poem would not be there,
chunky or clinking, fleshed from empty air.
It is like a good marriage: the man will know
the true wifely agreement from the say-so.
At times he will sulk, or shout, or practice disgust:
whichever seems to offer the most
likelihood of the hoped-for answer
to the non-questions it is impossible to ask her.
The tact is the keeping of a balance—
if that is what ensures, always, another chance.
Discounting nothing—kitchen trivia, boredom,
and the dreams of escape that make a home.

Flights

As a child I was fortunate
in having the gift of flight.
Many familiar streets and bodies
was I able to view from eight feet
above ground level; many conversations
and quarrels I observed secretly
(being invisible).
I did not think it unusual.

Youth crippled the gift somewhat.
Only on certain nights
in cold, unpleasant dreams,
housebound and lapped by evil
airs and murmurings, did I float
like a grotesque balloon
over snoring sleepers,
and down draughty, threadbare stairs.

By eighteen I could not rise at all,
but—as though in compensation—
dead relatives, and earlier
occupants of the house
began to make themselves known to me.
The unloved—an asthmatic aunt,
two weeping second cousins,
a bearded suicide, and a baby

that choked on a boiled sweet—
all made importunate demands
I lacked the experience to
satisfy, or even to understand.
When I started writing poems

they stopped visiting me,
except for Uncle Harry
who insisted that he was my guide,

and under this pretext
succeeded in writing the memoirs
he had been revolving in his head
for twenty-five years
in the County Mental Hospital.
He was a man with eyes
like the winter sun's reflection
in two dust-laden windows;

I was glad to see him gone.
In mid-life I neither fly
nor receive the frustrated dead.
The days are women's baking smells,
and the demanding cries of children.
The nights, when they are broken,
are broken by flesh, and the sleepy moans
of my children learning to master flight.

On the Cliff

Between the scented soap works
and cloud-capped cooling towers,
I walked one summer evening
swishing the soot-stained flowers.

Below, the black river
snaked around the racecourse,
drudging to distant sea
the dregs of commerce,

and huge across my vision
under the streaky sky
from Chapel Reach to Pomona Dock
the changing city lay,

swarming invisibly
with its intricate, restless hordes
of common humanity—
the keepers of the Word.

All I have accepted
to exercise heart and wit:
the unpredictable home
of the ever-unlikely poet.

There on the shifting cliff
where nothing built will stand
(local eruption of a fault
that runs across England)

I watched the lights come on,
and listened to a lover

coaxing a silent girl
under near cover,

and farther off the yells
of children at some chase:
voices much like my own—
the accent of the place.

The accent of the place!
My claim to a shared load
of general circumstance
with the hidden multitude.

Yet strange, despite the wish—
because my chosen task
was the making of poems—
I shivered in the dusk:

aware that my shining city
did not care one jot
for me as its celebrant,
or whether I wrote or not.

I might have been unborn,
or else long dead,
but before I reached my home
I had perfected

the sociable, lonely poet,
a rueful one-man sect,
in an ignorant, ugly city—
his God-given subject.

Approaching Bolton

Between the bridge and Moses Gate
close herbage blurs, we are flat out—

right on the governors. I imagine
something coming down on the same line.

Not really. For me, the leisurely bath
spoilt by the phone that stammers death,

the walk through trees to the cleaned-up site
of the gas chambers, the newsreel shot

of thousands of nameless bodies piled—
flesh burned away or disembowelled—

into mass graves somewhere else.
The stunned survivor's sense of guilt.

*   *   *

It is just an ordinary Tuesday
in mid-life; the same old journey

to earn my money, and back again
this evening on the stopping train.

Away to the left the town's sewage
settles through umpteen kinds of sludge

into a highly valued fertilizer,
and water that is officially pure.

Some have killed themselves, or gone mad
wearing the age's evil like a hood

they could not budge. The lucky man
staggers beneath his obscene burden

of luck, yet—sickened by common sense—
is glad of his life in a quiet province,

teaches his little children kerb-drill
although his nightmares are terrible.

* * *

Away to the right houses are going up
on the eminence of a filled-in tip.

The train stops at the scheduled platform,
I walk into town again without harm.

The Gamekeeper's Dotage

When he was eighty-two they opened
the first of the Supermarkets
on the main road. I don't think
he even noticed the mighty pyramids
of tins and washing-up liquid
at cut prices piled in the window—
although one Sunday morning
he caught in bare hands
the panful of boiling peas
that tipped from his black hob.
The house was silent and dirty;
it stank as if death were there already;
you couldn't be sure in rooms
where you peered as though through water
that hadn't been changed for years.
Of course, you never stayed long (the stench,
the dinginess, the look that showed—
again—he didn't know who you were),
but let him for his pride's sake brew
a pot of tea, and mumble for a while
among his towering memories, which
towards the end came down to one.

It was troubling to visit him by then;
to step from the main road's redevelopment,
the loaded shopping-bags, the lines
of shining cars, into that hush
where over and over he lifted arms
like trembling sticks, pulled the trigger,
and killed it for the Duke—the last
stag on the great estate
that has been a public park for fifty years.

Kon in Springtime

The Russian landlord who lets next door's
once carefully cared-for rooms to any-
body, is angry about the money
that's gone from his desk. He doesn't mind whores,
or coloured students, or jailbirds,
or kids. He trails to the 'bins in a tatty
dressing-gown—up at seven-thirty,
shaking his aristocratic head

at the evil in men. I like sharing
the area with him: revolutions,
pogroms, years in a concentration
camp, haven't made him despair
of human nature. He won't call the police
(he never does), or tell the suspect
to get his paper-baggage packed—
and he *isn't* liberal-minded. He'll curse

rotten the dirty bastard who
robbed him, and make life unpleasant,
deliberately, for all his tenants
for at least a day, and perhaps two.
But can't keep it up—he carries his years
gaily: the bow-tie, and the collar
of astrakhan are popular
sights in every local bar,

and at sixty-three, it's said, he still
has charm to enjoy the guarded virtue
of good wives, who open their legs to
nothing else that isn't legal.
May I survive a barbarous age

as well! Muttering, and miming punches,
under a clear blue sky he crunches
back to the door across the spillage

of cinders from his pail. I watch
from the kitchen table, where I've sat
all night, struggling to be a poet
in mid-journey at masterful stretch
among the rich imperatives
of family life. The Russian pauses,
staring at me as though my house is
haunted—reluctant to believe

I'm up at such an hour. He comes
worriedly to my window, certain
I must be awake because of children:
"Is it bad-sick, your little ones?"
he asks. I reassure him, they
vomited, but are asleep again.
He beams—who has never heard of Pushkin—
and says "It will be a lovely day."

New Place

Muffling our gasps of lust
trucks without mufflers
shift gear on Route 9.

Their headlights sweep the room;
we are two thrashing
ghosts as they rend past
going somewhere as fast
as the country road
will allow.
          We lie back,
going nowhere, waiting
in dense black
for the next truck's passing.
Our foreign white flesh
on the all-American
maplewood floor resists
every parable I begin.
In the approaching roar
shadows shape and lengthen.

Here there are new rules
to be learned. We appear
disappear, appear, as the night cools.

Walking by Birchwoods

The moon like a slippery secret
comes clear of the humped hills.

I am returning from the laundromat
thinking about the dead,
as though that watched turbulence of cleansing
had dislodged discreet spirits.

The least of them knows me too well;
some of them are my spitting image
and kick the snowbanks as I do,
whistling the latest tunes through clenched teeth.

Not that they come to accuse;
merely to remind in Massachusetts.

My old amiable companions!
Insulted, hurt, ignored—no matter,
they are glad to see me doing so well:
for whom else did they die?

My burden is children's clothes in pillowcases.

See those shimmering shapes dismember
at the first car's headlights!
Into the dark wood they scurry:
dried snow blown by the night wind.

The moon follows me mildly down the valley.

The Attack

Into the mind's emptiness
come thoughts of sickness:
the body, the brain choking—
agony-end of everything.

Consciousness narrows.
The pounding heart's slow blows
assume midnight. The room
throbs like a struck drum.

There is nothing, nothing at all
to be done—the attack is fatal.
Ears whine, nausea drags
sideways, beneath wild legs

the floor shakes; full moon's face
is a doctor, helpless,
watching nerves sever
eyes go out mouth slaver.

Then you are back, complete,
not knowing the half of it,
but magically healed
to a ponderous night-world

of cricket and frog sounds,
far wars and near wounds,
while sundry small thoughts purr
into a certain future.

Something has won something,
for what it is worth. Your strong
being prowls through the house.
The moon is anonymous.

In the Locker Room

Everything's clean and jolly:
genitals, butt, and belly
show with a nakedness
that causes none distress.
Between the locker rows
heaps of abandoned clothes
lie like a beaten race
crumpled in its disgrace.
All's cheer above—the Lords
of muscle-power and words
tingling from gym and joke
relax for a quick smoke.
Glad to be back again
in this clear world of men
I banish from my mind
the dark thoughts of its kind.
I rub my itching balls:
the seed of criminals
and maniacs waits
in those hanging fruits.

Flu at the Sheraton-Chicago

Channels of smudgy faces
ride upon the one unvarying voice:

Bad breath bad guys deodorants and death.

The bulk-bought furniture,
the personalized paintings, the selection of magazines
in the rack lie stunned in the room's heat.

If I force the venetian blinds
in a sudden panic, I will sense through aimless dense
snow the real world:
                      Metropolis where the judgements
of commerce take grey desirable shape.

Out in the dark
the Great polluted Lake crackles its icy fringe.
Slender white horizontals thicken upon the skeleton
of the tallest apartment block in the world.

My pill is like a parody of the bright spot:
the last embarrassed girl and the last corpse
being flushed away.
                      I gulp it down.

My sleep is haunted by the faithless multitudes of America.

Demonstrations of Affection

1

In dreams
I have seen you for what you are:
the mouth of Hell—
a cunt agape to receive the damned.

Laughing
you remind me too.
You are going to engulf me,
of that I am sure.

No wonder you must fondle me often
No wonder you must kiss me for nothing
No wonder you must reiterate how much you love me.

Being the unwilling possessor
of such deadly orifices.

2

You have not heard me.
Again
you have not heard me.

One day I shall speak
with Godlike crashes
from my black clouds.
Lightning will shrivel the children,
the kitchen floor will split
revealing
corpses I have not decided on yet.

I'll give you something
to pretend ignorance of.

3

You have gone to bed, tightlipped and elegant—
as to your death before me.

I sit listening to a Mozart quintet,
trying to invent a girl I first heard it with.

4

It is a long time since we spoke
to each other in simple terms.
Now it is difficult, unless one—waking
before the world assumes its weight—
catches the other murmuring in sleep
and, thinking little of it, answers
from a mind unpondering.
                              By day
our sentences rake to the world's end,
as though there were nothing
each had not a stake in the other would not steal.

You say "I threw that broken box away."
My grunt knows the enormity of the act.

5

Wiping
the smell of women
from my hands

74

and loins,
I am fidgety with words.

In the upper darkness
her sleep
has already begun.

Wordlessly it flows
through the house
oozing my juices.

6

Veteran of many wars,
how you confuse me!
Your apparent guilelessness
leads me to a gunpoint.
And when I am taken prisoner
you protest ignorance:
"That's your idea" you say,
"I don't even have a cheque-book."

"Such sophistry" I think
as I visit other women.
By your casual magnanimity
set free.

Listening to Bach in Franklin County

The police in the cities prepare for summer,
there is much talk of the need for order.

A fugue in the wilderness
ravishes the hearts of a few impotent men.
With lunatic fastidiousness
the music steps from my window
towards the scrub forest before
and the Shopping Plaza behind,

inviting assassination—
such fervent benevolence open to the night air.

It all happens again:
                          the just go down,
the greedy, the stupid.
                          Battlefields
become the pastures of scholars.

One thinks of ways to preserve one's sanity . . .
fugues whose structure one only senses,
a political sticker on the windshield
that partly obscures one's vision.

The forfeiture of giant miseries
                                    to write
a small poem at midnight.

Morning Song

This northerly light is bleak;
bedrooms should face south.
The mirror claws your cheek
like time itself; your mouth

(how often moved to kiss
its image of pretty glass?),
puckered and bloodless,
drops open on "Alas!"

Archaic, tragic, tall,
your strong form gathers in
from a million bedrooms all
the grief of beautiful women.

Every ageing body
outraged by morning light
you don for lonely study—
symbol and anchorite.

And I, a tousled fool—
not meant to understand,
except in poems—recoil
as if from a large demand

I cannot answer, although
you don't so much as glance
towards me and my show
of sleeping ignorance.

My operatic dear,
lost in your noble part—

sombre, nude, bizarre,
no live man's sweetheart—

descend to feed the children:
assume the debased forms
from which flow affection,
abuse, domestic storms,

for these I can well gauge,
and grapple with something more
than frightened patronage
(now pretending to snore).

Names on Stone

In old graveyards
I could wonder what mattered.
All those particular names
affect me like a starry sky.

Who was a good man?
Who cheated many?
Who greeted each day with a song?
Whose life was one long pain?

Tumours, palsies,
hare-lips, hunch-backs
are gone with kindness
and the odour of sanctity.

Some evidence of riches remains,
and of poverty; but both
soon become part
of the same official care.

If you go back far enough
even the most stubborn accumulations
lose all meaning.
Stones hold names

like stars. You look,
and around you
the emptiness deepens
with everything named that no one knows.

An Anonymous Painting

In a tessellated courtyard a young lady
is teaching a dog to beg. A child
plays with a ball. An aged servant
drying her hands on a gathered apron,
looks out smiling upon the scene
from the door of the house. The walls of the courtyard
(mellow red brick, about ten feet high)
are partly obscured by trailing woodbine
of a colour which suggests summer is over.
The light, too, has the glow of withdrawal,
though it dwells with the amplitude of eternity
upon cracks in the tiles, the dog's tongue,
the smooth neck of the lady, and the shoe
peeping from beneath the child's dress.
Above the courtyard the land falls away
in strangely tilted perspective that shows
the buildings, towers and spires of the city
the courtyard is part of, and—beyond—a landscape
where a drunken-looking peasant ambles aimlessly
towards a small copse on a small hill,
and two workers absorbed in their task
lift scythes to standing grain in a field
sprinkled heraldically with neat stooks.
Farther off is a sea, empty of ships,
and farther off still—where the trembling blue
distances curdle into frilly mountains—
comes on, in a descending glitter of highlights,
the minute beginnings of the monstrous army
that will conquer, loot, and sack the city.

II

New Poems

A Short Account at Fifty

I was conceived in the black
of midnight and ignorance.
No more of a true romance
for being out of wedlock.

I fell to earth in a town
smoke-dingy, stinking of wastes.
Echoes of Great War *Last Posts*
reminded me of dead men.

A new war broke out. I crouched
in a shelter underground.
It seemed like the threatened end,
but peace came, drizzling and botched.

Adulthood tugged at my balls:
now I was a Serviceman:
"Army of Occupation"
they called us—boys full of boils.

Demobbed, and back in England,
I slept, ate, worked, went back to bed.
Labouring for small reward:
could such dullness be demeaned?

By degrees I found my heart
was master of prick and pen:
I married and had children,
I sat at a desk and wrote.

Years passed. The blink of an eye
turned my wife into ex-wife.

I shook the marriage-mud off,
and found myself high and dry

in a most unlikely place,
Middletown, Connecticut.
Here I recall, or forget
my various histories.

And dally in middle age
with what frightened me in youth,
dissipating in good faith
a Methodist heritage.

Look for me on a barstool,
or in some kind woman's bed,
talking hard, and undismayed
by folks who think me a fool.

Or see me in the evening
sedate and gravely amused
to find myself once more faced
with a poem on the wing.

Not that the world has improved
as my understanding's cleared:
monstrously base, savage-bored,
it snarls at me to be loved,—

no less than when I was born,
many years and miles away:
the careless, proxy by-blow
of young men killed on the Somme.

Sunday Afternoon: Heaton Hall

FOR MARJORIE BOULTON

"They're not *real* cats," my sister
said, her lips pressed to the glass
that separated us from
the tiny, silent kitchen.

"Don't be daft—of course they are!"
I said, lips almost as close.
"They've been killed, and emmed with balm,
and dressed like men and women."

"Ugh!" she said, flouncing away,
"I think it's quite disgusting"—
and catching sight of a school-
friend through the huge bow window,
she ran from the room to play
in the rose-garden, among
the cheerful crowds who would fill
the park until the horn blew
for the closing of the gates
at sundown.
            An attendant
stuck his grey face into mine
and lectured me about noise
as soon as she'd gone. "But it's
not fair!" I said, "It wasn't
me, it was *her* who ran!"

"You're pests, you bloody young boys,
I'd clear out the lot of you
if I had my way," he said.

He gave me a guarded shake,
and hobbled off to caution

a youth who was about to
tap the top of a bronze head
of Palmerston.
                    This new trick
of my sister's—having fun
and letting me pay the price—
was not one I liked at all.
As I examined the cat-
tableaux in their glass-fronted
scaled-down rooms, I thought of ways
of asserting my rightful
mastery: of proving that
a nearly-ten-year-old lad
could always get the better
of a sister not yet nine;
but the motionless tabbies
and toms, staring sightlessly
at one another over
cups of tea, and games of gin-
rummy and chess, seemed to tease
from my mind its brotherly
ambitions.
              There were about
twenty cases in all—each
depicting a different
domestic scene. *The Bankrupt*
showed a drawing room, ornate
and richly furnished, in which
a portly, pompous Merchant-
Prince stood tragic and erect
against the fireplace as he
told his wife and small children
of his ruin. The tom's striped
expression somehow conveyed
a world of business worry
above wing-collar, silken
tie and black suit. His wife wiped

a tear from her eye, and tried
to comfort the two kittens
in frilly dresses who knew
that something was wrong, and were
hiding their furry faces
in their paws.
                    Most of the scenes
were happy, though:—the tableau
called *A Party Below Stairs*
made me laugh out loud. The case
was crowded with alley cats
dressed as chambermaids, butlers,
cooks and so on. One lay drunk,
a wine bottle in his paw;
others wore saucepans as hats;
some were dancing the Lancers;
some flirted; some swilled down drink.
In the middle, on a chair,
stood a disreputable
moggy with one eye missing.
He looked like a gypsy, and
was scraping from a fiddle
the silent music that filled
the room.
                    Somewhere a bell rang,
and soon I heard the raw sound
of the horn rasping from hill
to boat lake, to rose-garden,
to landscaped hill.
                    "Now sod off,
sonny," the attendant said,
"We're closing in five minutes,
and if I catch you laughin'
at them exhibits and stuff
again, you'll be blacklisted,
and not let in!"
                    His bright boots

twitched, as though he would have liked
to kick me from the Hall, but
he made do with a fierce glare,
so I stayed with the cats
a moment, before I walked
into the foyer and out
of the enormous front door.

The rose-garden was empty
when I reached it—except
for a cripple with two sticks
plodding towards the far gate.
Then, from the back of a tree,
my sister appeared and slapped
some roses into my fist.

"Hide these under your raincoat,"
she said, "They're for mam."
                              "You've pinched
them!—You were hiding!" I said.

"I was just having a pee,
Clever!" she said,—"Look: I'm wet."

I punched her and strode off, hunched
over flowers and hatred.

On the bus she said sweetly:
"They weren't *real* cats—what d'y bet?"

Invalids

Whether the wintergreen smelled
of antimacassars, or
the antimacassars smelled
of wintergreen, I don't know.
Both, I imagine—those rooms
were too small for things to keep
individual presence;
too small and too full of sleep,
and sickness, and silent hours
brooding upon life and death.
From where I sat the pot dogs
stared out from the tarnished glass
on the mantelpiece (the rooms,
my visits, all seem the same),
the flowers on the blanket
drooped in bunches to tangle
with the carpet's threadbare blooms,
and the great sepia stag,
in the sepia forest,
under the sepia sky,
yearned, full of admiration,
for the lion on a field
of Union Jack leaping
colourfully from the lid
of the assorted-biscuit
tin being offered to me
by the old man or woman
smiling on the stacked pillows.

How long had those invalids
been lying in the front rooms
my grandma used to visit,

leaning on me and her stick?
What were they bedridden for?
And who were they—apart
from people she knew? Not one
has a face I remember.
Not a word comes back to me
of the talks about old times
they must have had with grandma,
or the polite enquiries
they probably made of me.
Nothing comes back but the smell
of wintergreen. Every
other detail—(like the lace
runners, the pokerwork plaques,
the fake-marble fire-surrounds,
the gas brackets, brass bedsteads,
bottles of medicine, spoons,
brown bakelite wirelesses
and small change on bedside stands,
that I hadn't intended
to mention) is enlisted
for the sake of this poem—
which might otherwise be vague,
and maunderingly shamefaced
at so many small sickrooms
so thoroughly forgotten.

Grandma and the Blitz

My grandma sat on the bed,
spilling over the edge
like a huge lump of dough.
Her eyes looked already dead,
her mouth dropped long beads of spit
onto her grey nightgown:
one glance and I was off—
sure she was having a fit.
I was only ten, and wrong
about a lot of things:
who Mr. Chamberlain
was, why Germans yelled "Achtung!"
how many guns the Spitfire
carried inside each wing;
but I was nearly right
about grandma—the doctor
said she had suffered a stroke.
My mother sent me out
to play, and for three days
hardly bothered me or spoke.
I was glad to be alone—
those were exciting times,
with bombers on their way
and most of the children gone
from the city to seaside
and country. There were air-
raid shelters to explore,
barrage balloons overhead,
a strange anti-aircraft gun
under camouflage nets
in the park, and no school
to interfere with my fun.

Some time after grandma died
the children drifted back
and the city was blitzed.
"Thank goodness your grandma's dead,"
my mother sighed one cold night,
as we crouched in the dark
of the cellar with bombs
exploding to left and right,
"This would have killed her." The past
didn't interest me;
I was impatient for
the "All Clear," and then breakfast,
and then the morning treats:
swastika-marked tail-fins,
and shrapnel and shell-shards
picked from the smoking wet streets.

A Photograph of My Mother with Her Favourite Lodger

Looking at these loved faces—
his above a limp bow tie,
hers beneath a flowered hat—
I try to catch their voices
from thirty-five years ago,
and I can never do it.

Except in dreams, and then I
am a shy uncertain boy
listening amid uproar
to grand sounds of poetry,
while air raid sirens nearby
shriek out a too late Beware.

He is mangling bits of *Lear*
and the *Rubáiyát*, large hands
sawing the air, gargoyle face
twisted as though on a sour
taste, oblivious to bangs
of guns and bombs, and to us.

She is boiling with disgust:
"The fool's showing off again,
what are you listening for!"
I am his captive, held fast
by a strong incantation
of which he is not aware.

This scene didn't take place
in fact, although he *was*
our lodger during the war,
and he *did* first come to us

through flattened streets and smashed glass
when the city was on fire.

No: it is my sleeping mind's
gaudy vision of the Child-
hood of The Poet, replete
with frightening figures and
destructive detail. Beguiled
I may have been by the fruit

of that raucous Yorkshire voice,
scarred I certainly was by
my mother's sneering hatred
of things beyond her small house—
but it all happened slowly
when I was a growing lad.

I'm sure he uttered his last
misquotation long ago,
and my son lost her ashes
while I was in Budapest
in Nineteen Seventy Two—
they're both as downright dead as

they're ever likely to be
in my lifetime. What remains
is for me to hear them right:
worrying querulously
the same few mouldy old bones
as I became a poet.

In Crumpsall Library

Under the great Byzantine dome
were all the books in the wide world,
ordered and numbered on dark shelves;
and there was a long reading-room
with leathered tables at which lolled
vagrants who came to warm themselves
and ponder on the morning's news,
or study ancient magazines.
The place seemed to ask of me more
than the church where I went to praise
a God I didn't believe in,
and all those faces—like a choir—
gleaming from the stained glass windows:
Shakespeare, Homer, Cervantes, Keats,
Milton, Gray, Euripides, Burke,
looked down upon me with kind eyes—
kinder than the martyrs and saints
staring from the walls of the church—
or so I thought. I was thirteen,
the library a new-found land
a mere cock's-stride from my home street.
Every day when I had done
my paper round I would ascend
the marble steps (flanked by unsweet
chasms leading to the public
conveniences—on the right
the "Ladies," on the left the "Gents")
and with quick breath and burning cheeks,
as though I were trespassing, flit
past the spectacle-flashing glance
of the lady at the counter
and on into the shadowed hush

of the stacks. I wanted to read
every book to be found there;
but I meandered in a lush
dream of knowledge among the dead
and the living, sorely afraid
that I could understand nothing.
Whether it was the serene gaze
of the noble band in mid-air,
or the hawking and loud yawning
of the vagrants in a half-doze
over their papers, I'm not sure;
but something put me at my ease,
and I was soon lost to the place
in books I couldn't understand.
A bomb blasted in the stained glass
windows one midnight. The faces
meant particular words I'd found
and read by then: no one was hurt.
Later there was a daytime raid
while I was in the library
thinking vaguely about the church
that I no longer attended.
I was skimming through a book called
*Secular Modes of Religious
Experience* when the sirens
started wailing. A flapping-soled
vagrant tripped, and threw me a curse
as we hurried to the basement.

My Mother Singing

My mother sang: "There's a long,
long trail a-winding into
the land of my dreams," and steam
came drifting up with the song
from the cellar-boiler she
stood over, filling rooms
and corridors with odours
of wet washing. Her Monday
chore took hours and hours: sometimes
she was still at it downstairs
when I arrived home for tea—
water sloshing and dull rhymes
thumping. "Where the nightingale
is singing and the bright moon
beams." The songs were always from
the trenches of Passchendaele
and the Somme, where the young men
she might have married became
corpses she couldn't mourn. Now,
over twenty years later,
she had been long abandoned
by the stunned survivor who
gave her two children, and there
was another war to end
war, and she took in washing,
and no young man dreamed of her
as he dozed in a dugout;
but she was fit and strong,
and who could say what was fair
or what life was all about?
I am putting thoughts into
the head that sings in my head—

a man the age she was then.
In truth I will never know
why she sang, and she is dead,
like all her lovely young men.

Desertion, Doom, and Mistaken Identity

Before Tiskoffs came next door
a newly married couple
rented the house: the Cohens.
She was beautiful (so I
heard my mother say to my
Auntie Doris) "for her sins";
he was a big man called Phil,
who soon went off to the war.

She was related somehow
to the Goldbergs up the street,
and used to go out a lot
at night with Brenda Goldberg,
another grass-widow, fur-
coated and spindly-heeled. "What
their husbands would say I hate
to think!" seemed like an echo

I never caught the source of.
Then—among all kinds of things—
everybody heard that
Phil Cohen had deserted
from a posting in the Med.
Mrs. Shindler discussed it
with my mother while broad wings
of wet washing flapped above

in the smoky breeze that blew
straight along our narrow back.
And all the other women
had ideas, too: "He's heard
of her carryings-on; word

must have reached him in Aden
or what's the name of the rock,
Gibraltar?—I ought to know."

I heard them gossiping at
yard-doors as I went about
my games and errands. But soon
they returned to rations, raids,
Tommy Handley and small kids;
as though Mrs. Cohen's doom
(quickly approaching) were not
one with their virtuous spite.

Was I so perceptive when
I was eleven years old?
Thirty seven years later
and four thousand miles away
I would laugh at any guy
who asked. Or would I say: "Sure;
we were bombed; many were killed;
it made adults of children"?

Which reminds me of the Yanks
I used to see emerging
from next door—Army Air Corps
sergeants, rushing back to camp
at Burtonwood in the damp
early-morning air before
the part-blacked gas lamp went "Ping"
at the gate, and gave three blinks

and went out. "She must be mad,
man-mad!" I heard my mother
telling my Auntie Lucille.
"God help her when *he* gets back;
he'll soon stop her little tricks,

if he doesn't maim or kill
her or something or other.
She'll wish she'd not heard of bed!"

But Phil didn't return, and
she didn't change her bold ways.
Not that I cared greatly what
grown-ups did or didn't do,
as long as they left me to
the secret life of croft, street,
entry and ginnel—the maze
of the district, with its blind

alleys and sudden vistas
where bombs had opened long views;
still, when Mrs. Cohen *did*
meet her doom, on a cold day
about ten months later, I
was thrilled and horrified.
Trying to make a fire blaze
in her kitchen grate she was

burned to death when her nightgown
went up in flames. The police
who came to her funeral
were on the lookout for Phil,
I heard Mrs. Shindler tell
my mother. "What sort of fool
do they think he is, to chase
after the slut now she's gone?"

The Tiskoffs, Morris and Bel,
moved in after the kitchen
had been repaired. She was plain;
he was Unfit for Service,
a bald, bowlegged man with

flat feet. They used to moan
at each other all the time—
we could hear them through the wall.

An age later, when I thought
of little but my next chance
with Shirley Hoffman's bare breasts
in her mother's dark front room,
I was standing in a dream
one night with my risen lust
big in my pocket. No hints
escaped the houses of light

within—the back where I lurked
beside the air-raid shelter
was still Black-Out dark. Some twigs
tickled my face: they hung down
from the tabernacle lean-
to Mr. Mantel had rigged
beside his yard-privy for
Succoth. Then, out of the dark,

two giant shapes came at me
and pushed me against the bricks
with their chests. "You are Cohen,"
one of them said. "No! Connor,"
I said. "Cohen," the other
said. "Connor," I said again.
"Cohen"—"Connor"—"Cohen"—six
or seven times the silly

antiphon was repeated.
"We are detectives," one said.
"Well, I am only fourteen,"
I said, frightened. "I live *there*

with my mam." "So you're Connor,
eh?" the other said. "Well, run
off home—you should be in bed.
Go on, now, there's a good lad!"

A Moment in Adolescence

Near the railway embankment
on an evening in July
when I was just turned fifteen
I had a revelation.
A low, invisible sun
shafted light upon the scene
from a cloud-infested sky,
and four men fixing a tent
in a hayfield to my right
ambled off towards the town—
one whittling an alder branch.
I squashed a worm with my foot;
there came a hidden child's shout
"I'm not playing if you pinch!"
As for the revelation—
I cannot remember it.

A Face

Catching it in shop windows
I'm always mildly surprised
by the fixed, ferocious scowl
it gives me back: as though praise
were something to be refused
on any terms, any scale.

Arranged for its owner's view
it is more amenable
to compliments and kind thoughts.
The level look seems to say:
"I acknowledge I'm a fool,
but not the worst hereabouts."

Then there's its passionate life—
which I'm sure I'll never know:
how it behaves in private
when I forget it in grief,
anger, terror, pity, joy,
or feeding an appetite.

Sometimes I awake to blind
lips puzzling its stubbled cheek,
fingers tracing its forehead;
as though it were neither owned
nor remembered in that dark,
where all social selves are shed.

But mostly it's on display
in politic, daily guise,
to make a good impression.
Perhaps you've seen it, and know
its affable, worldly ways?
I've only you to go on.

Reminiscences Remembered

FOR F. K.

"It must have been the summer
of '28. Fordie had
taken me to visit one
of Proust's minor Duchesses . . ."

The old poet, another
tale begun, nodded his head
as though in confirmation
of a better time than this—
and I thought we and the place
no more than mist on a pane
through which he gazed easily
backwards on youth and greatness.
Now, speaking from Olympus
himself, he did not disdain
the greedy questions and sly
notetaking of those whom booze
had made unmannerly, nor
did he sneer at the breathless
student poet who said: "Wow!—
you actually *knew* Yeats?!"
Better to say he showed no
marked interest in *Tiny's
Modern Café*, and the young
faculty members who'd lured
him there to bask in the glow
of his reminiscences—
although it was ferreting
Americans who'd flattered
him from his forgotten hole
in northern England onto
Olympus and SUNY at

Buffalo.
          "Yes, Eliot
didn't hit it off at all
with Isadora. He threw,
or tried to throw, Ezra's goat
from the window of her flat,
as a gesture of protest
at Isadora's neatness.
I should say 'her studio'—
which was bare, completely bare;
as—so it must be confessed—
was 'Dora, who greeted us
in the hall stark naked!"
                    Now
someone replenished his beer
in the reverent silence;
a Black Mountain person
asked a question about Pound's
understanding of *breath-pause*.
The old poet looked askance
at the glass he'd just put down,
and said:
          "Cat's-piss!—which reminds
me of that cat Willie was
always fondling: Minnaloushe.
'used to pedicure its paws,
claimed it had psychic powers—
especially after it peed
all over George Moore's valise
stuffed full with reams of his prose.
I got the tale from Arthur.
—Symons: he witnessed the deed."

I didn't stay till the end,
knowing that later he would
be persuaded to comment

on the *Cantos*, and his part
in them, and then condescend
to lift his own book and read—
or utter in mannered chant—
the measured words of his art.

His private being, shrunken
and myopic, occupied
the apartment next to mine—
where, sometimes, I'd visit him.
With memory fixed upon
himself among the great dead,
the rest of his mind would strain
nobly to deal with the dim
fellow-countryman he saw
in the room. Once, speaking with
a patrician politeness,
he said:
   "I daresay that now,
the future of poetry,
of poetry in English—
if it has a future—lies
with unschooled fellows like you."

He followed this with some
words in a foreign language
unfamiliar to me:

"Which, to be more accurate
than Fitzgerald—if more lame,
I translate as:
   'Jamshýd, Mage
and Master, in the windy
ruins of your Peacock Court
an ignorant tribesman sings
as he kindles his dung-fire.'"

It was not for me to laugh
at the self-serving fictions
that give poetry its wings,
so I passed him a fresh beer,
lowering my head as if
put in my place and chastened.

He endeared himself to me
by late summer: he refused
to allow the library,
or anybody, to tape
his reminiscences.
                    "No,
my boy: I won't have them *used*.
Damn these university
confidence-tricksters, in lip-
service to literature!
They want articles, footnotes,
anything in black and white
that'll help 'em get tenure.
I'll see the sods in hell-fire
before they transcribe my thoughts
and ramblings into their neat
effete books on *Belles Lettres*!"

He'd flushed such a fearsome red
that Gertrude Stein's description
of him did not seem inapt,
or even caricatured.
I saw us both reflected,
like grotesque father and son,
in the mirror that said *PABST*,
where Tiny stood embowered
among pewter mugs, bottles,
girlie posters and joke cards.
The old poet shook his head,

as though to be rid of flies.
He popped a couple of pills
into his mouth, muttered: "Turds!"
saw me beside him, and said:

"There are lies, and there are lies.
What you'll remember of me—
years from now, in some pub, say,
or perhaps in a poem,
speaking from the pure pleasure
of telling a good story—
will be warped, changed, pulled awry
into your own idiom.
You'll soon make *my* stories *your*
stories—that's how it should be.
Murrain take accuracy!
Speak with a rich man's freedom,
leave facts to the sober poor!"

The Crowd at My Door

Many people who are dead
address me within my head,

some with a vague nod and smile
as we pass at a turnstile,

some with familiar words
from beside kitchen cupboards.

Others are more troublesome:
they hover outside my home,

ambiguous, bold and sly,
waiting to importune me.

They grip my arm, and bluster,
they run fingers through lank hair,

they laugh, cajole, threaten, weep,
like actors in third-rate Rep.

They call me "Love"; "Sir"; "You swine";
"Bud"; "Holiness"; and "Bo's'n."

I can't find out what they want,
or why they choose me to haunt,

or who each one thinks I am—
for none of them knows my name.

And they keep switching titles,
as though all were death-rattles—

one as good as another:
"Dad" a ghost moans, then "Mother."

When I question them they grow
wild-eyed with wordless sorrow;

when I sweep them to one side
they clamour loudly "Coward!" . . .

"You broke my heart!" . . . "I sinned!" . . .
"The women and children drowned!" . . .

"Kiss me!" . . . "Intercede!" . . . "Forgive!" . . .
"You do not know how to love!" . . .

I can't have them arrested—
no policemen walk my head—

so I bear their harassment,
their obscure, riddling intent;

although I stay home for days,
all shades drawn against their eyes.

Seven Domestic Poems

To the Unwary Reader

Do not study these verses
thinking to find me in them.
I hurried out to follow
old friends leaving in hearses,
and am not expected home
till they pay me what they owe.

My feelings are well hidden,
unreachable and remote.
I disowned them in childhood
and threw them on a midden:
all roads leading to the spot
have been declared closed for good.

Nor shall your like discover
what meanings I mean to share.
I speak from a dark closet,
where I fondle a lover
whose flesh is dust, and whose bare
bones sharper than my sharp wit.

Bringing in the House-Plants

A few of them are foundlings—
here's one I picked from a pot
someone had smashed on the street—
but most of them were given
with pictures and other things
unwanted, or not quite worth

space in a U-Haul. A north
wind blows: now they must live in.

I should have moved them sooner;
perhaps I wished for a frost
to come like a silent ghost,
one night while I was asleep,
and kill them off? I prefer
to believe I've been harassed,
busy, with no time to waste
on thinking of their hardship:—

(Committee meetings, the young
making new demands, women
forcing into the open
this and that and the other . . .
"If I've done anything wrong,
I'm sorry," I said to her.
"Oh, that's always your answer,"
she said—just like my mother.)

Anyway, these plants don't seem
to have suffered, although dead
leaves blown from the part-naked
trees lie thick around them, all
over the porch. In the dim
rooms of my house they won't thrive,
but I'll give them enough love
to ensure their survival.

If "love" is the right word for
daily fussing and fretting
over *Snake Plant*, *Gossip's Tongue*,
Wandering Jew and the rest
of the bastardized creatures.
I don't know why I keep them—

unless it's their obscure claim
to be my wards, and my guests.

Emptying the Fishtank

First the algaed plastic plants
are eased from their holding stones
and dumped in soapy water,
then the decorative shells.
    Lifting the sunken vessels
is trickier: they splatter
the counter with blobs like blains
on gangrenous flesh—their joints
oozing a vile sediment
as I swing them to the sink.
    Next the goldfish must be caught
(where they blunder frantically
through an element, thickly
clouded with I-don't-know-what
stirred-up matter) and dropped, *plonk,*
plonk, plonk into a new haunt—
the old zinc bucket waiting
on the floor to receive them.
    The entire operation
takes about ninety minutes,
and depresses my spirits
with its insistence upon
the universe as a slum
that can't be kept clean for long;
nevertheless I always
recover my good humour
before it's done—perhaps by
seeing myself from the point
of view of a fish, or (faint
but swelling) by hearing high

hosts of angels in a choir
Magnifying Me with Praise.

Taking a Bath

When I was born I arrived
trailing clouds of misery,
whose slow evaporation
has left me at last naked,
and ready to be beloved
by the obscure deity
who watches such things happen,
though they spring from his own head.

As a child, youth, and young man,
I hated getting undressed:
the bathtub was a low place
where I averted my eyes
from the corporal human
encumbrance, that shat and pissed
and did other things much worse,
which I could hardly surmise.

With age the misery's gone.
I sit here pleased and amused
by the sharp, female fragrance
that still clings to my upper
body, and was sharpest on
the primary organ used—
now lolling like a tired prince
half-asleep in warm water.

I've got two nakednesses mixed,
but no matter: my bathtub-
speculations at fifty

dream away demarcations
till nothing's discrete or fixed—
the flesh and spirit hobnob,
and women and God both say:
"Quiet—that room's the children's!"

Not Cleaning the Windows

Which poet was it that thought
poems should be transparent—
much like panes of window-glass
which don't attract attention
to themselves unless some flaw
makes the prospect they present
seem blurred, bent, or otherwise
distorted and part-undone?

I don't know. But he left out—
I dare say circumspectly—
the coating of dirt and dust
that builds on every window
to obscure and cast in doubt
the point of the simile,
because it may be erased
in favour of a clearer view.

Still, I carry a bucket,
a squeegee and sponge-mop,
and I'm high up a ladder
with a lot of work to do—
this is no time to speculate
on poetry, I may drop
something, or come a cropper
on the concrete path below.

What's more, I must insist on
windows remaining windows
if I'm to finish my task
of washing and polishing
back, sides, front, upstairs, and down,
every last pane in the house
before the onset of dusk,
or the beginning of spring.

I've postponed it for so long
(seven years, to be exact—
since I first came to live here!)
and still I procrastinate,
babbling on with double-tongue
as though I were in the act,
while I bang the typewriter
and try to keep my thoughts straight.

Making a Din with the Vacuum-Cleaner

Telemann could never have
imagined what would happen
to his music. All those years
of mute burial, and then
a bursting up from the grave
to appreciative cheers!

Still, he was a wise old bird,
who tried to please the patron,
and succeeded. No doubt that
was enough. Wouldn't unborn
patrons have been an absurd
audience for him to court?

Good artists don't make bequests
to the future. Shakespeare went

with a shrug of foul papers:
he knew nothing could prevent
his voices shrinking to ghosts
who'd squeak bleakly in Hades—

or lexicographers' minds,
to abandon metaphor.
And long before the final
snuffing-out (whether by war,
or live wastes breaking their bonds
in some deep ocean channel)

householders reading *Hamlet*
to Telemann's music, will
obliterate both to groom
living-room, kitchen and hall,
so that the place will look neat
when next week's visitors come.

Listening to the Heating System

More ominous than a ghost
in the cellarage, the sound
of the furnace turning on
interrupts my play of thought—
already under attack
from pains in the leg and back.
How to work a poem out,
with that infernal machine
chunnering of OPEC and
what this winter's warmth will cost!

It's an old story, all right:
family, and politics,
and ills the flesh is heir to
bring many a noble mind

to its knees (the metaphor
is mixed:—my knee-joints are sore).
Shall I renounce my first bond,
and send the children away?—
rent a smaller house?—buy stocks
in Oil, and go corporate?

Of course not; I'll soldier on
paying monthly heating bills,
and grumbling about the size
of this wide, three-storied house,
while I try to write good verse,
and my arthritis gets worse.
No lunges at the arras—
I lack the wild miseries
that construct their own death cells;
mine is an open prison.

Touring the Premises

Someone has padded talcum-
powder all over the house;
or are these a ghost's footprints?
Aimless peregrination
it seems to me, as I track
the spoor down the back stairway
from the bathroom (where it starts)
to the kitchen, and across
the living-room carpet
into the hall. Following
the milky, translucent marks
up the front stairs, I find them
entering all the bedrooms:—
what's going on here? I think;
is there some promiscuous
spirit abroad in my house—
are my next-door neighbours
correct in their suspicions?
I'm sure they'd say: "Without doubt!"
finding thickly-spread powder
in front of the toilet bowl—
where one of my teen-age sons
dusted his bathed and dried flesh
with half a cannister-full
of talc,—and realizing
that fourteen feet have spread it:
broadcasting private journeys
as though the many were one.

A Small Annoyance

The Italian's pigeons
sit on the telephone wire
outside my bedroom window:
I am wakened by the row
from their ragged, cooing choir
long before the day begins.

All summer the fat old man
potters about his green yard
among tomatoes and vines;
to complain of his pigeons
would brand me as ill-tempered—
they are his senile passion.

So I curse them in private,
and wave to him as I weed
my struggling vegetables.
Three houses away, he smiles,
and strokes a held pigeon's head
before urging it skyward.

Stud, Hustler, Penthouse, et al.

These acres of nakedness—
what do they mean? These calm girls
fingering their private parts
open for the dullard's gaze
in drug-stores, and the self-toils
of young boys without sweethearts?

Sometimes a rigid penis
lurks in the vicinity,
while a well-manicured hand
resolutely exposes
the viscous, pink mystery
from which we all come death-bound;

but most often these girls lie
as though the world were remote,
and aroused men a daydream
spawned by their fingers to sigh
and grunt in some foreign state
at a photograph of them.

It is done for the money,
and ignorantly, no doubt.
Meanings are not their business:
the photographer's O.K.
sends them out on a lunch-date,
or to shop for a new dress.

Nor are meanings *my* business—
I should have an erection,
to stop me thinking so much
of this abundance of flesh,
which is not meant to question
lust, loneliness, love, and such.

In New York City

Silences no traffic's roar
can muffle steal out like smells
of childhood from the backs of
eyes fixed on *Do Not Walk* lights
and meters showing cab-fares.
They are heavy; they are full
of dead people and old words:
words spoken and forgotten,
words misremembered, and words
that were never used at all.

This is a certain moment
moving, between birth and death,
towards an evening's revel.
Soon apartments are unlocked,
drinks fixed, phone-calls made to friends;
and now—safe from strangers' eyes—
in silent, scented bedrooms,
young women fresh from showers
examine the ferny vein-
patterns on their inner thighs.

Music on a Summer Night

Surely that's a piano
piece by Bartok the police
siren's rising and falling
wail is cutting across. No:
I am wrong. It is a waltz
called—I think—"Voices of Spring,"
by Archibald Joyce. But why
should I mistake a string band
for a solo piano?
Perhaps the humidity
and heat are to blame—my mind,
like my flesh, is feeble, slow,
and reluctant to engage
in active intimacies
with the world beyond this room,
or even beyond this page.
But the curtains stir and rise
towards me across the prim
disorder of my desktop,
then, sucked by a hot night-wind,
drag my eyes into the dark,
as they belly out and flop
against the window-screen. And
there, full of students and talk,
is the house with the music—
across the street, with nothing
between us but moonless night
brimming with the brainless creak
of crickets. "Voices of Spring,"
I recall, is by Strauss; that
is not the tune, nor is Joyce
the composer. What is more,

now I think that the siren
was an ambulance. It was
no doubt rushing to a fire,
or heart attack, or the scene
of a terrible car crash.
Of course, one cannot be sure—
for that matter there might be
someone desperately rash
practicing at your front door
"I'm going to have your baby."

The Voices

It is not a litany;
most of the time there is no
response, or there is a sigh
or a mumble or a slow
sobbing like someone alone
with a grief beyond sorrow
in the next room.
                    Then the phone
rings, and it is the living
with demand, invitation,
advice, or full listening
silence—nothing like the deep
self-absorption of the long-
dead.
        Sometimes when I'm asleep
they will speak in the voices
of distant trains, and the drip
of late raindrops from roses,
and the sigh of wind-stirred trees
at the back of the houses;
but these are merely echoes
telling me of things I know:

"In winter the ground will freeze."

"I studied all day today."

"The frying pan is greasy."

"High is high and low is low."

Aubade

"Mr. Nobody," I thought,
when the bedroom door rattled
scattering my pleasant dream
of childhood. The dawn light boomed
and soughed as the wind battled
trees and houses in the street;
already the hammers were
declaring their flat dogmas
in Wilcox and Crittenden's
Marine Hardware factory;
already the whining roar
of the garbage truck, zealous
in its crushings and grindings,
was waking sleepers nearby.
"Mr. Nobody," I thought,
wrapping my dream around me
(or was it the bedcovers)
and I was far from lovers:
their bold comings, their sulky
goings—their sly-passionate,
guarded goings at first light
or whenever. I was back
in *A Child's Garden of Verse*,
and in the child reading it
a long time ago. I thought
later (when I was awake
enough to acknowledge her
fading imprint on the sheet,
her scent on the pillowcase)
that I did not know her name,
or what she had been doing

in my room. Such are the strong
resistances I bring home
from all my acts of darkness.

Lost Love

I was thinking of lost love,
or trying to think, across
the bad-mouthing of my heart
(which would not stop its insults),
and a pop-song about love
drivelling from somewhere close
to the chair in which I sat
waiting for a girl whose faults
I was not yet aware of.
   It was a busy lunch-hour
in the Delicatessen;
but I was trying to think
of a time and place and love
vanished into the thin air
of what cannot come again,
so my mind kept going blank.
   The best that I could manage
were a few vivid day-dreams:

making love through her wild tears
just after her mother's death
("She should have been on the stage,"
my heart said); the blue-veined domes
of her nursing breasts; the stairs
with the baby's crib beneath;
her anger when she found out
my worst infidelity
("You were always a lecher,"
my heart said); the way she smiled
one night in kitchen firelight,
after I left my study

and came to confer with her
on making another child.

("*This* is thinking of lost love?"
my heart said—or the spirit
of the Delicatessen),
and a man with a tray
gave me an impatient shove
as he sidled to a seat.
"Oh honey, do it again!"
sang the pop-group from L.A.,
then I saw my latest girl
shaking the snow from her hat
near the door. From a distance
she looked like Zenobia,
or some undismayable
Goddess; but she was too late
to catch me as I was once—
not that she would have liked me.

A Weekend Incident

A date in January,
but the morning warm, spring-like:
blue sky with a few white clouds,
squirrels dashing jerkily
between the trees, and two Psych
majors fulfilling their needs
by hurling a frisbee to
and fro in front of my house.
"A nice day in a small town"—
even the hullabaloo
of ambulance and police
cruisers on some near mission
didn't change my opinion.
Then, into the street they bombed,
terrifying the squirrels
and scattering Mike and John—
whose frisbee flew to its doom
under a cruiser's rear wheels.
To be honest, by the time
I got out of the basement
and onto the stoop the scene
was orderly, the street calm.
But something seemed imminent
in front of Number Eighteen,
where the empty ambulance
and cruisers stood in a yawp
of unanswered transmissions.
I walked down on the off-chance
that my neighbours, closely grouped
on the sidewalk, might make
sense of it all for me. John said
Eighteen was a student-house:

perhaps someone had O.D.'d?
"Yeh, I guess some young guy's dead,"
added the gloomy recluse
from the corner. Mike had heard
there'd been a fight. The woman
with Our Lady in her yard
recalled a sour cop grumbling:
"Goddam vibrators again"—
but there was no certain word,
and I went back to mopping
up the mess of last night's flood
in the basement, where many
stored objects had been ruined.
Later on I decided
that, though the day was now grey,
I'd walk to visit a friend.
At the door I collided
with the mailman, who said: "Shit!
where are you going so fast?
It's a shame about that kid
who hanged himself down the street.
There's a foot of snow forecast."

Middle Age

Call it a settled habit
after twenty years or more—
this sitting in the evening
with a blank page before me,
waiting for words that might
tell me what I mean. I fare
badly most nights: phones ring,
doors slam, the lodger's hi-fi
thumps its bass down through two floors,
my daughter comes for a kiss
before bed, my sons to get
the keys to the second car;
but still I persist. For hours
I sit here in bored distress
listening to a debate
taking place in the mind's ear—
a debate about nothing
and everything, the secret
subject of which is rarely
identifiable in
the babel of stammering
voices. Sometimes I forget
my responsibility,
and don't listen. Then a stain
on the edge of the blotter
takes me back to the kitchen
of my childhood, or a smell
curls from nowhere, and again
I'm well-married to her
whose body, cool and open,
moves beneath mine as I feel-
out the form of a poem.

"And leave the voice of commerce
blaring through an empty house"

I wonder how much remains,
now that I've used my last lines—

or what I *thought* were my last,
even though they arrived first?

They seemed designed to fulfill
a short, riddling parable

to do with life in my home,
and its eventual doom;

but the sibyl hardly spoke,
and I've no power to fake

true sibylline utterance,
if it doesn't come at once.

Why bother to write at all,
with no mouthing oracle

at the ear of my study,
where I sit at the ready?

Reduced to a man of sense,
why need I nurture silence?

More useful to emulate
the folks next door, Fran and Dwight,

whose loud FM receiver
misses no bargain offer,

who rush to far discount stores
in their end-of-year-sale cars,

and leave the voice of commerce
blaring through an empty house.

Notes

St. Mark's, Cheetham Hill
The word *gollop* is not in common use in England, except in the north, where I come from. It means to swallow greedily or hastily.

Elegy for Alfred Hubbard
In Lancashire and Yorkshire a *ginnel* is a narrow roofed passageway between houses in a row.

A Journal of Bad Times
A *pike* is a tower built on the summit of a hill.

Mayor Isaac Watts
This poem deals with my ancestors, many of whom came from Gloucestershire. The word *didicoy*, meaning a gypsy or a vagrant posing as a gypsy, is used in their part of England, not mine.

The Poet's District
A *brew* is a steep cobbled slope. A *croft* is a piece of unused land between buildings, or a vacant lot where a building once stood.

Approaching Bolton
In England the officially sponsored method of teaching small children to cross the road is called *kerb-drill*: "Stop! Look left. Look right. If the road is clear proceed with caution."

Desertion, Doom, and Mistaken Identity
Tommy Handley was the most popular comedian in the British Isles during the Second World War.

A Short Account at Fifty
In the British Army, *Last Post*—or Lights Out—is the bugle call sounded at the burial of a soldier.